CD INCLUDED

DRUMS

HAL•LEONARD
BIG BAND
PLAY-ALONG
VOLUME 7

Standards

T0101507

ISBN 978-1-4234-5889-0

HAL•LEONARD®
CORPORATION
7777 W. BLUEMOUND RD. P.O. BOX 13819 MILWAUKEE, WI 53213

Visit Hal Leonard Online at
www.halleonard.com

Standards

AUTUMN LEAVES

English lyric by JOHNNY MERCER
French lyric by JACQUES PREVERT
Music by JOSEPH KOSMA
Arranged by PETER BLAIR

DRUMS

From BORN TO DANCE
EASY TO LOVE
(YOU'D BE SO EASY TO LOVE)

DRUMS

Words and Music by COLE PORTER
Arranged by SAMMY NESTICO

THIS PAGE HAS BEEN LEFT BLANK TO ACCOMMODATE PAGE TURNS.

GEORGIA ON MY MIND

Words by STUART GORRELL
Music by HOAGY CARMICHAEL
Arranged by MARK TAYLOR

DRUMS

HARLEM NOCTURNE

Music by EARLE HAGEN
Arranged by JOHN BERRY

DRUMS

From STATE FAIR

IT MIGHT AS WELL BE SPRING

Lyrics by OSCAR HAMMERSTEIN II
Music by RICHARD RODGERS
Arranged by MARK TAYLOR

DRUMS

JA-DA

Words and Music by
BOB CARLETON
Arranged by SAMMY NESTICO

DRUMS

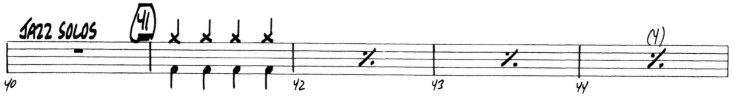

From BELLS ARE RINGING
JUST IN TIME

Words by BETTY COMDEN and ADOLPH GREEN
Music by JULE STYNE
Arranged by SAMMY NESTICO

Drums

From BABES IN ARMS
MY FUNNY VALENTINE

Words by LORENZ HART
Music by RICHARD RODGERS
Arranged by SAMMY NESTICO

DRUMS

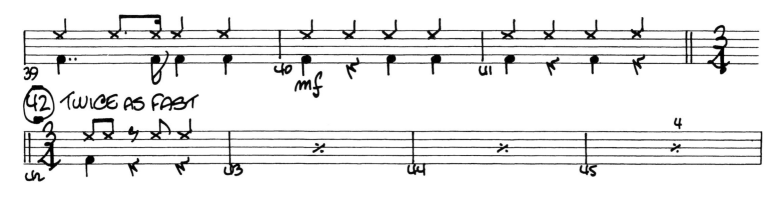

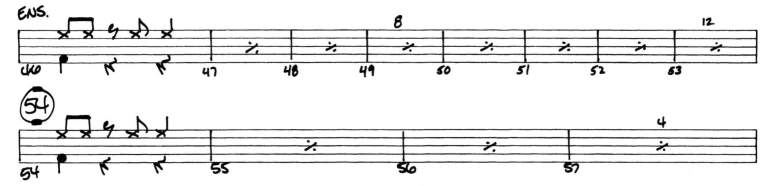

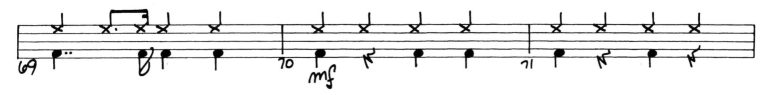

From GOLDEN BOY

NIGHT SONG

Drums

Lyric by LEE ADAMS
Music by CHARLES STROUSE
Arranged by RICK STITZEL

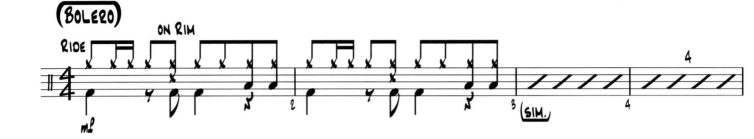

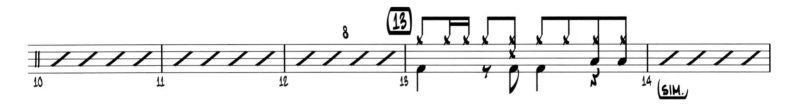

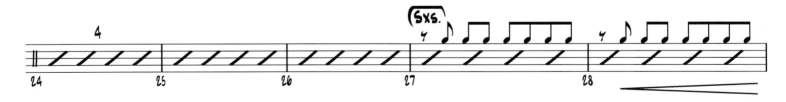

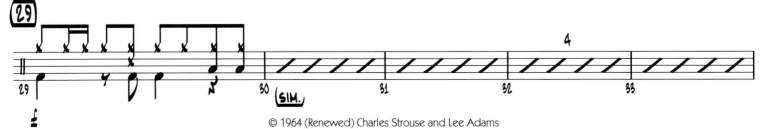

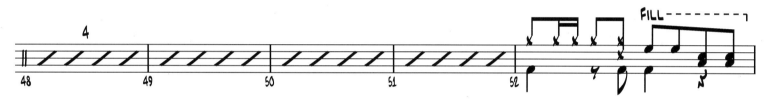

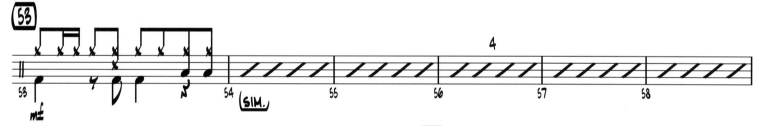

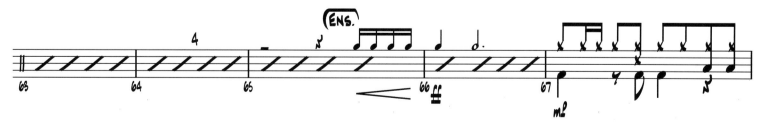

ON THE SUNNY SIDE OF THE STREET

Lyric by DOROTHY FIELDS
Music by JIMMY McHUGH
Arranged by SAMMY NESTICO

DRUMS

YOU CAN'T BEAT OUR DRUM BOOKS!

Bass Drum Control
Best Seller for More Than 50 Years!
by Colin Bailey
This perennial favorite among drummers helps players develop their bass drum technique and increase their flexibility through the mastery of exercises.
06620020 Book/Online Audio $17.99

The Complete Drumset Rudiments
by Peter Magadini
Use your imagination to incorporate these rudimental etudes into new patterns that you can apply to the drumset or tom toms as you develop your hand technique with the Snare Drum Rudiments, your hand and foot technique with the Drumset Rudiments and your polyrhythmic technique with the Polyrhythm Rudiments. Adopt them all into your own creative expressions based on ideas you come up with while practicing.
06620016 Book/CD Pack $14.95

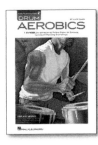

Drum Aerobics
by Andy Ziker
A 52-week, one-exercise-per-day workout program for developing, improving, and maintaining drum technique. Players of all levels – beginners to advanced – will increase their speed, coordination, dexterity and accuracy. The online audio contains all 365 workout licks, plus play-along grooves in styles including rock, blues, jazz, heavy metal, reggae, funk, calypso, bossa nova, march, mambo, New Orleans 2nd Line, and lots more!
06620137 Book/Online Audio $19.99

Drumming the Easy Way!
The Beginner's Guide to Playing Drums
for Students and Teachers
by Tom Hapke
Cherry Lane Music
Now with online audio! This book takes the beginning drummer through the paces – from reading simple exercises to playing great grooves and fills. Each lesson includes a preparatory exercise and a solo. Concepts and rhythms are introduced one at a time, so growth is natural and easy. Features large, clear musical print, intensive treatment of each individual drum figure, solos following each exercise to motivate students, and more!
02500876 Book/Online Audio $19.99
02500191 Book $14.99

The Drumset Musician – 2nd Edition
by Rod Morgenstein and Rick Mattingly
Containing hundreds of practical, usable beats and fills, *The Drumset Musician* teaches you how to apply a variety of patterns and grooves to the actual performance of songs. The accompanying online audio includes demos as well as 18 play-along tracks covering a wide range of rock, blues and pop styles, with detailed instructions on how to create exciting, solid drum parts.
00268369 Book/Online Audio $19.99

Instant Guide to Drum Grooves
The Essential Reference
for the Working Drummer
by Maria Martinez
Become a more versatile drumset player! From traditional Dixieland to cutting-edge hip-hop, *Instant Guide to Drum Grooves* is a handy source featuring 100 patterns that will prepare working drummers for the stylistic variety of modern gigs. The book includes essential beats and grooves in such styles as: jazz, shuffle, country, rock, funk, New Orleans, reggae, calypso, Brazilian and Latin.
06620056 Book/CD Pack $12.99

1001 Drum Grooves
The Complete Resource for Every Drummer
by Steve Mansfield
Cherry Lane Music
This book presents 1,001 drumset beats played in a variety of musical styles, past and present. It's ideal for beginners seeking a well-organized, easy-to-follow encyclopedia of drum grooves, as well as consummate professionals who want to bring their knowledge of various drum styles to new heights. Author Steve Mansfield presents: rock and funk grooves, blues and jazz grooves, ethnic grooves, Afro-Cuban and Caribbean grooves, and much more.
02500337 Book $14.99

Polyrhythms – The Musician's Guide
by Peter Magadini
edited by Wanda Sykes
Peter Magadini's *Polyrhythms* is acclaimed the world over and has been hailed by *Modern Drummer* magazine as "by far the best book on the subject." Written for instrumentalists and vocalists alike, this book with online audio contains excellent solos and exercises that feature polyrhythmic concepts. Topics covered include: 6 over 4, 5 over 4, 7 over 4, 3 over 4, 11 over 4, and other rhythmic ratios; combining various polyrhythms; polyrhythmic time signatures; and much more. The audio includes demos of the exercises and is accessed online using the unique code in each book.
06620053 Book/Online Audio $19.99

Joe Porcaro's Drumset Method – Groovin' with Rudiments
Patterns Applied to Rock, Jazz & Latin Drumset
by Joe Porcaro
Master teacher Joe Porcaro presents rudiments at the drumset in this sensational new edition of *Groovin' with Rudiments*. This book is chock full of exciting drum grooves, sticking patterns, fills, polyrhythmic adaptations, odd meters, and fantastic solo ideas in jazz, rock, and Latin feels. The online audio features 99 audio clip examples in many styles to round out this true collection of superb drumming material for every serious drumset performer.
06620129 Book/Online Audio $24.99

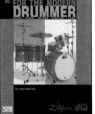

66 Drum Solos for the Modern Drummer
Rock • Funk • Blues • Fusion • Jazz
by Tom Hapke
Cherry Lane Music
66 Drum Solos for the Modern Drummer presents drum solos in all styles of music in an easy-to-read format. These solos are designed to help improve your technique, independence, improvisational skills, and reading ability on the drums and at the same time provide you with some cool licks that you can use right away in your own playing.
02500319 Book/Online Audio $17.99

HAL•LEONARD®
www.halleonard.com

Prices, contents, and availability subject to change without notice.

1221
022